LIFE
AMERICAN SPEED

Lee Petty, in a '54 Chrysler New Yorker,
flies across the sands of Daytona Beach;
previous page: Barney Oldfield rides to
glory in Beverly Hills; following pages: cars
blur in the 2000 Coca-Cola 600 in Charlotte.

LIFE
AMERICAN SPEED

From Dirt Tracks to Indy to NASCAR

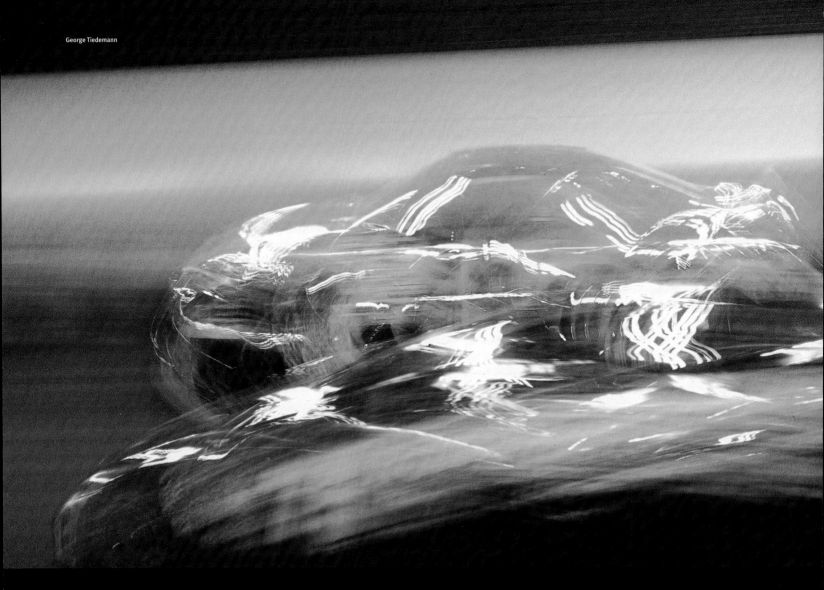

George Tiedemann

LIFE

Editor Robert Sullivan
Creative Director Ian Denning
Picture Editor Barbara Baker Burrows
Senior Editor Robert Andreas
Associate Picture Editor Christina Lieberman
Senior Reporter Hildegard Anderson
Copy J.C. Choi (Chief), Stacy Sabraw
Production Manager Michael Roseman
Picture Research Lauren Steel
Photo Assistant Joshua Colow
Consulting Picture Editor (London) Suzanne Hodgart

Publisher Andrew Blau
Director of Business Development Marta Bialek
Finance Director Camille Sanabria
Assistant Finance Manager Karen Tortora

Editorial Operations Richard K. Prue (Director),
Richard Shaffer (Manager), Brian Fellows, Raphael Joa,
Stanley E. Moyse (Supervisors), Keith Aurelio,
Gregg Baker, Charlotte Coco, Scott Dvorin, Kevin Hart,
Rosalie Khan, Po Fung Ng, Barry Pribula, David Spatz,
Vaune Trachtman, Sara Wasilausky, David Weiner

Time Inc.
Home Entertainment

President Rob Gursha
Vice President, Branded
Businesses David Arfine
Executive Director, Marketing
Services Carol Pittard
Director, Retail & Special Sales
Tom Mifsud
Director of Finance Tricia Griffin
Marketing Director
Kenneth Maehlum
Assistant Director Ann Marie Ross
Prepress Manager Emily Rabin
Associate Product Manager
Jennifer Dowell
Assistant Product Manager
Michelle Kuhr

Special thanks to
Suzanne DeBenedetto, Robert Dente,
Gina Di Meglio, Anne-Michelle Gallero,
Peter Harper, Natalie McCrea,
Jessica McGrath, Jonathan Polsky,
Mary Jane Rigoroso, Steven Sandonato,
Bozena Szwagulinski, Niki Whelan

Published by

LIFE Books

Time Inc.
1271 Avenue of the Americas,
New York, NY 10020

Library of Congress Control Number: 2002106437
ISBN: 1-931933-19-7

"LIFE" is a trademark of Time Inc.

We welcome your comments and suggestions
about LIFE Books. Please write to us at:
LIFE Books, Attention: Book Editors,
PO Box 11016, Des Moines, IA 50336-1016

If you would like to order any of our hardcover
Collector's Edition books, please call us at 1-800-327-
6388. (Monday through Friday, 7:00 a.m.–8:00 p.m.
or Saturday, 7:00 a.m.–6:00 p.m. Central Time).

Please visit us, and sample past editions of LIFE,
at www.LIFE.com.

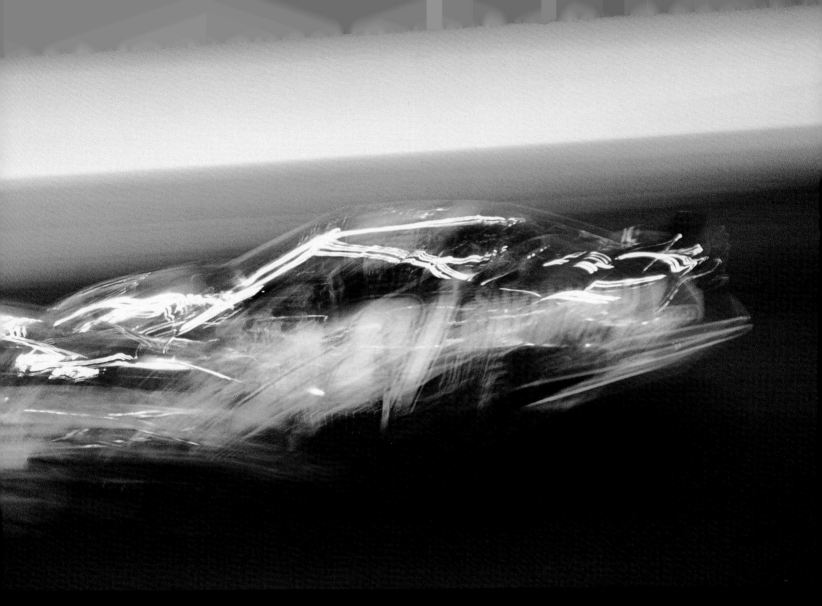

6	Introduction by Mario Andretti	76	An American Classic
10	The Starting Line	80	Dynasty: The Pettys
20	Legend: Barney Oldfield	84	Legend: A.J. Foyt
22	Indy!	86	Stars and Cars
32	Dynasty: The Chevrolets	92	The Rise of NASCAR Nation
34	Off the Beaten Track	106	Dynasty: The Earnhardts
50	Dynasty: The Andrettis	110	The Fans
54	NASCAR!	114	In the Pits
64	Legend: Junior Johnson	118	Crash!
68	Dynasty: The Unsers	122	In Victory Lane
72	Women at the Wheel	128	Afterword by Jeff Gordon

AN AMERICAN DREAM

Introduction by Mario Andretti

In 1947 the Andretti clan poses in Montona: matriarch Rina, patriarch Gigi and the children, from left to right, Mario, Anna Maria and Aldo. The following year they would return to their native Italy, but not, yet, to better days.

It was the newsreels. During intermission at the movie house they would show newsreels of the Grand Prix, and my brother and I would watch those wonderful cars and the great champion, Ascari—Alberto Ascari. He was my hero. Aldo and I would study the newsreels and then talk about nothing else for days. It's not only what we wanted to do; we wanted to be Alberto Ascari. When you're a kid, your dreams have such grandeur, and realizing dreams is so far away. But they were our dreams nonetheless.

This was in the early 1950s. Aldo—my twin—and I had been born on February 28, 1940, in Montona, Italy, near Trieste, but our family's situation had changed a lot since then. During the war, there was always a danger that my father, who managed seven farms, might be killed—or that any of us could be. The situation under the Nazis was chaotic, and then, after the war, Montona became part of Yugoslavia, and so was ruled by the Communists. They ruled the town, the farms, us. In 1948 the conditions became impossible and we had to leave. We ended up in a refugee camp in Lucca, Italy, for seven years. Our family of five lived in one room of an abandoned school, blankets separating us from the

other refugees. We were not starving or cold or anything like that—just existing. It was a hard time, but I believe your foundation makes you who you are. It gives you a frame of reference. It forms your future.

It was there that Aldo and I fell in love with cars, through newsreels and magazines. There was a garage in downtown Lucca where we hung out when we weren't in school. The garage was always packed and we were allowed to park people's cars in these tight rows. Oh, man, if they could have seen what we were doing to their cars. Spinning around, not hitting anything, but trying to come within an inch. We had a ball.

Then, in 1954, the fellows who owned the garage took Aldo and me to the Italian Grand Prix in Monza. Ascari and Juan Manuel Fangio fought each other all day. Ascari lost, but we were thrilled anyway. From that day on, it was clear. This is what we wanted to become.

Now, all the while, my dad was determined to move us to America. He had put in a request for U.S. visas a few years earlier, and we had been waiting and waiting. Then, suddenly, our visas came through and my parents gave us the news—we're moving to the United States. My brother and I were devastated. No more Ascari. No more racing. Our life was over, we were sure. Boy, were we wrong.

An uncle in Pennsylvania helped bring us over and we settled in his town—Nazareth. The very first weekend we were there, Aldo and I heard a loud rumble and spotted these lights on the outskirts of town. It was the Nazareth Speedway, a half-mile dirt oval that had been built in the '20s. Stock cars were roaring around, unlike anything we had ever

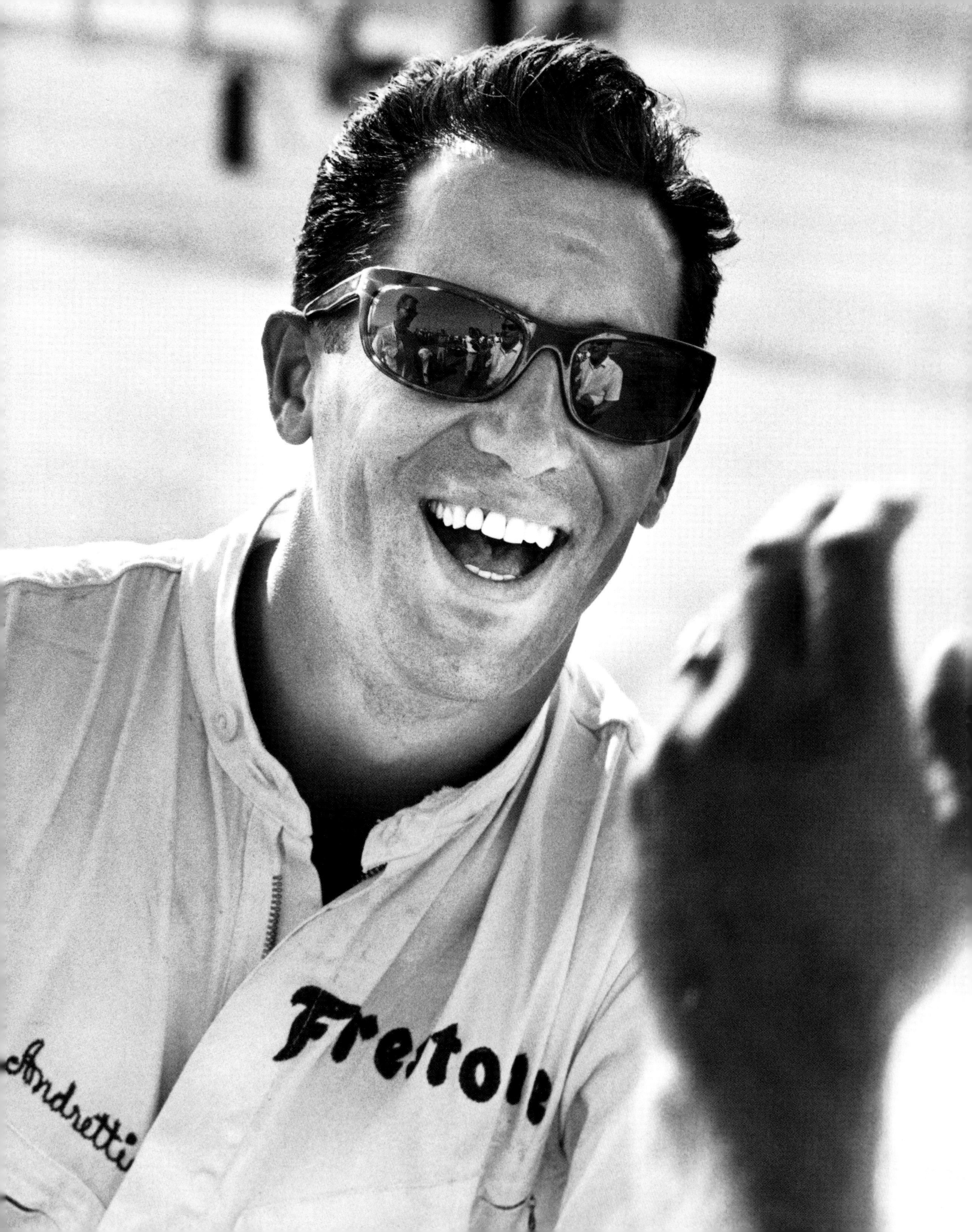
Andretti

seen. I stared at them in fascination and knew then what was possible. You see, Ascari and Formula One were so grand and impossible, even if I didn't realize it. This, in Nazareth, was something that Aldo and I could attain. I was sure of it.

We set goals. We gave ourselves half a year to learn English, and we did it. Next we were determined to race. Working part-time at a gas station, we began saving money so we could build a car. The Hudsons were doing well at NASCAR races and I liked the looks of them a lot, so we got a few friends together, pooled our money and built a '48 Hudson coupe with parts from a scrap yard. We were ready and anxious, but only 19 years old, and you had to be 21 to race. It was hysterical the way we finally got onto the track. All the racers in those days wore T-shirts and jeans and just tore around the course. But Aldo and I had bought these racing uniforms, one blue and one white, and we showed up one night all dressed up, with our red-painted car. We lied about our age and said we had raced in Italy since we were 13. Some of them laughed, but they let us in.

Because they didn't know anything about us, we had to start last in the heat. Aldo and I flipped a coin and he won the toss, so he got to drive first. I stood there watching as Aldo came right through the field, went by everyone and won his heat. Same thing in the feature race, right by everyone and he wins. I won my first race too, and that was the start of it—roaring and banging in stock cars at the Nazareth Speedway in 1959.

The brothers and their buddy and benefactor Bob Noversel hang at the Nazareth gas station in 1959. In '78 an earlier legend, Fangio, waves Mario home in the Argentine Grand Prix.

Why do I tell you this, and what does it have to do with the history of car racing you hold in your hands? Well, I can promise you that all of the drivers in the pictures you will find here had similar dreams about this sport, this passion. I have often said that my family, in every sense, was able to experience the American dream—and that is true of many others in racing.

When I say that, I mean every kind of auto racing. People often ask me about Indy cars and Formula One and stock cars. Why did I drive them all, which did I prefer? From the beginning of my career, I wanted to be versatile so I raced midgets and sprint cars, which were the stepping-stones to Championship or Indy cars in those days. I knew I wanted to go to Indianapolis to win the 500, and I was lucky enough to do that. My growing relationship with Ford and Ferrari allowed me the opportunity to race stock cars and long-distance sports cars. I won the Daytona 500 in 1967. The NASCAR drivers were terrific and we got some of them—the Allison brothers and Cale Yarborough—to come to Indy and race there. In 1978 when I won the World Championship with Lotus, it was wonderful to be back where I had been as a boy, but now sitting in a thoroughbred just like Ascari did.

The truth is, I loved all of it. I loved it whenever I was behind the wheel in a fast car.

I am not a historian, but I think back on some of the great early drivers that you will meet in these pages. Ralph DePalma was winning in Indianapolis and setting land-speed records. Louis Chevrolet drove whatever he could, and so did Barney Oldfield. Some of the finest were my contemporaries: A.J. Foyt and the Unsers. Bobby Unser got me to try the Pikes Peak Hill Climb, where he and his brothers competed every year. He loaned me a car, then he beat me! He felt bad, and in 1969 he gave me his better engine and this time I won.

There are so many families in racing—the Pettys, the Unsers, the Earnhardts, our own—because, I think, it's especially easy to hand down something when you love it and talk about it and have great spirit about it. I never pushed my sons into racing, but they were always at the track with me. When other kids went to summer camp, they went to the track. It was no surprise when Michael and Jeff told me they wanted to race. The same with Aldo's sons, John and Adam. Now Michael's son—my grandson!—is driving karts. Who knows where the road will take

Mario (above) won more Indy car races than anyone except A.J. Foyt. His eldest son, Michael, seen below with Dad, has been one of the circuit's dominant drivers throughout the 1990s and into the new millennium.

Marco? Right now, he's just following his dream.

Yes, of course I worry. Tragedy lurks in the shadows. But I certainly wouldn't be the person to stop another from pursuing something he is passionate about. And the sport is safer now. When Aldo and I started to drive, there were, let's face it, a lot of people dying in motor racing. Too many. Things are so much better today, and getting better still.

Racing is in great shape right now, all of it is. Many of the best drivers in open-wheel racing are competing at the Indy 500 again because they know the prestige of winning this event. The popularity of stock-car racing has flourished, surprising, I think, even NASCAR itself. In Formula One, Ferrari's doing well again, and to have Ferrari strong is so important.

My dreams now? Well, in 1995, a year after I retired from active competition, I raced again at the 24 Hours of Le Mans. The weather was terrible all day and night. Our car had trouble early, so we played catch-up in the rain, and nearly got there. My team finished second, only three minutes behind. Le Mans is the one significant race I've never won. That trophy would sure look good on my mantel. Next year? Who knows? Anything's possible.

A Revolutionary Race in Rhode Island

The earliest racing in Europe and the U.S. was on the open road. But here, in September 1896, eight four-wheelers line up at a horse-racing oval in Cranston, R.I., for what will be the world's first track race. Five of the entries are gasoline-powered cars built by the Duryea brothers of Massachusetts, but stacking the field doesn't help. The winner, a daring driver by the name of Whiting, pilots his fleet Electric over the turf at an average of 26.8 miles per hour during the five-mile race.

THE STARTING LINE

They were off and chugging more than 100 years ago.

The urge to race is human instinct, and always has been. On foot, in chariots and on horseback, the games of the ancients sought to determine who was swiftest. The horsemen were, and for millennia it was assumed that they would be forever. But then, near the close of the 19th century, man turned on the ignition.

Almost as soon as inventors developed reasonably successful automobiles—not yet called that, but, rather, "motocycles," "quadracycles" and "horseless carriages"—drivers were champing at the bit to race them. Karl Benz and Gottlieb Daimler built the first reliable gas-fueled cars in Germany in the 1880s, and when Daimler brought one of his to the 1890 Paris Exhibition, the response was a rapturous "Ooh-la-la!" In 1894 a French news magazine, *Le Petit Journal,* sponsored a 78-mile reliability test from Paris to Rouen, and the trophy went to a Peugeot with a Daimler engine. The following year, Peugeot again took first place when it finished a 732-mile round-trip from Paris to Bordeaux in 59 hours. The gun had sounded for motor sport.

In the United States, meantime, many bright young men were in a race to manufacture workable autos on this side of the pond. The inventor John Lambert made a three-wheel car in 1891, the same year that William Morrison came out with an electric-powered vehicle and Charles Black debuted what he called a chug buggy. The Stanley twins, Francis and Freelan, tinkered throughout the decade with what would become their famous Steamer, and in Springfield, Mass., another set of brothers, Charles and J. Frank Duryea, were hammering on what would become, on September 21, 1893, the first gas-powered four-wheel American automobile. It was, in fact, a modest carriage with a one-cylinder engine attached, but this prototype was nothing short of a revelation.

Mimicking events in Europe, a newspaper—the *Chicago Times-Herald*—sponsored a race in 1895 offering $2,000 to the winner of a 54.36-mile out-and-back to Evanston. The next year, at a harness racing track in Cranston, R.I., something that looked even more like car racing as we know it today was staged: a five-mile race on a one-mile oval. The winner averaged over 25 mph. With that result, everyone at the horse track realized the animal's reign as King of Speed would soon be over.

A Brisk Beginning in Illinois

The *Chicago Times-Herald* sensed a growing interest in the automobile in 1895 but was astonished to receive more than 60 entries for its race to Evanston and back. The surprise extended to Washington, where President Grover Cleveland asked the War Department to keep order during the contest. Snow coated the ground when vehicles departed Chicago's Jackson Park on November 28 at 8:55 a.m. In hazardous conditions, only two finished. The No. 18 car and all others were no match for the Duryeas' No. 5, driven by Frank (in cap) at an average speed of nearly seven and a half mph. Thus did the coinventor of the first American car become America's first car-racing champ.

Brown Brothers

All Kinds, Coast to Coast

In the first decade of the 20th century, racing
swept the country. Right, on April 24, 1908,
roadsters traverse the hills and dales of
Westchester County, just north of New York
City, in the Briarcliff Trophy Stock Car Race.
It is the first race on average town and country
roads, giving an indication of what an auto
owner might expect in everyday driving.
Above, on March 13, 1910, they roar past the
grandstand at Ascot Park in Los Angeles during
a 100-mile event, the last dirt-track race staged
in L.A. (Ray Harroun won that day in one hour,
40 minutes; the following spring he would take
the spoils in the inaugural Indianapolis 500.)
Down in Florida in 1903, they started 32 years
of land-speed trials on the hard-packed
sand of Ormond Beach. Alexander Winton won
his friendly bet against Ransom Olds that first
year when he zoomed a mile down the beach at
a speed of nearly 60 miles per hour.

Gordon E. White and Joseph S. Freeman Collection

Brown Brothers

Man and Machine

Fred Marriott (above) set a world record in 1906 at Ormond in the Stanley Steamer Rocket. It looked like an upside-down canoe with four bicycle wheels, which, given its wood-and-canvas body, wasn't far off the mark. But it went 127.7 mph that year, helped greatly by its revolutionary sleek lines that set the driver down low for both speed and protection. Right: Savannah was a popular site in the early days. In 1908, Eddie Hearne in a Buick leads Lee Lorimer's Chalmers Detroit in the International Light Car Race. Ralph DePalma (below) won nearly 2,000 races, but he called his victory over Barney Oldfield in the 1914 Vanderbilt Cup his greatest.

Culver Pictures

Bettmann/Corbis

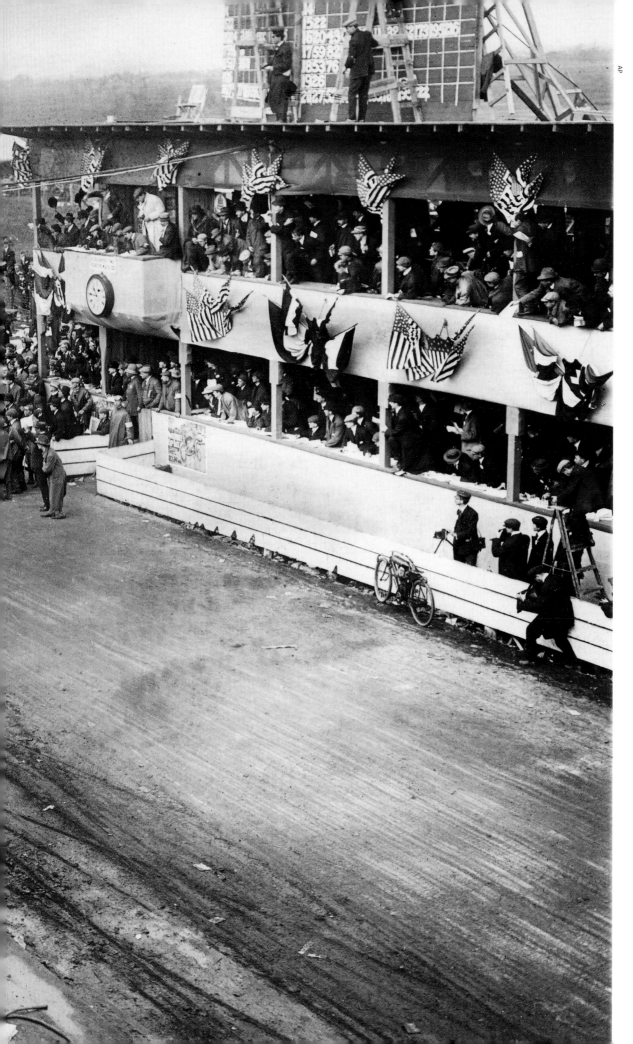

The Vanderbilt Cup

The most well-known American race prior to 1910 was the Vanderbilt Cup, brainchild of millionaire and sometime racer W.K. Vanderbilt Jr. Staged on the roadways of Long Island, N.Y., beginning in 1904, it was a wild and woolly affair as spectators—a quarter million on a nice day—lined a race route that was without barriers. "Directly in the road were at least 50 persons as we approached the turn," recalled Frenchman Louis Wagner, the 1906 winner. "They swiftly made way, but my car must have brushed at least a dozen coats while taking the turn." Two years later, American George Robertson takes the checkered flag in a Locomobile (left). Two years after that, the Vandy Cup was finished as a road race on ever more populous Long Island.

LEGEND Barney Oldfield

Culver Pictures

Brown Brothers (2)

In the early days of racing, cars were almost exclusively playthings for the wealthy. The men hired to drive those racers were routinely attired in what amounted to livery, in the manner of servants. But in 1902 a blow was struck for the common man when Berna Eli Oldfield was introduced to a fellow by the name of Henry Ford.

Born in 1878 to a hardscrabble Ohio family, "Barney" began working at an early age, as a laborer, bellboy, elevator operator. His goal was to be a salesman or a professional boxer (he practiced for the latter in saloons, a long-standing tradition throughout the land). He showed an early bent for speed as a competitive bicyclist, and it was another rider who brought him to Ford. The genius inventor had designed a car that was promising but too hard to handle, until Oldfield took the tiller and slid around the turns in a cloud of dust, which would prove to be a signature maneuver.

By 1903 he had become a top driver, and at the Indianapolis State Fairgrounds on June 20 he made history in Ford's 999 when he circled a dirt track in 59.6 seconds, thus becoming the first American to drive a mile a minute—*a mile a minute!* For years to come, Oldfield was synonymous with speed and daring, photographed everywhere with his sly grin and the cigar that he clenched between his teeth

even as he drove. Boys everywhere copied his cocky gait and round goggles. He was the Wizard of the Track, the Speed King of the World. It is certainly no exaggeration to say that he instilled in the average American a love for auto racing, which might otherwise have remained a rich man's affair, like polo and yachting. As for Ford, he once told Oldfield, "You made me and I made you." To which Barney replied, "I did a damn sight better for you than you did for me."

Oldfield set a Ruthian number of records, including the world-speed mark of 131.724 mph in 1910 ("the sensation of riding a rocket through space"). He retired from "organized" racing in 1918, although he would race tractors and so on for years. He would have notched many more wins had the lordly American Automobile Association not barred the free-wheeling Oldfield from their events. He was the very personification of an American racer. For decades, when a traffic cop pulled over a speeding motorist, he began the dialogue with "Who do you think you are, Barney Oldfield?"

INDY!

"Gentlemen, start your engines!"

They call it, simply, the Speedway. There are other speedways: a NASCAR fan will point to Daytona and Talladega. But in the world of racing, there has long been only one Speedway, capital S. The Speedway, which has been on the National Register of Historic Places since 1975, is, for the record, in Indianapolis, and the Indy 500 means Memorial Day at the Speedway.

The race and the place were purposeful inventions. Before car racing in America had reached its 15th birthday, there were already so many different and competing events that it was impossible, in the words of the famous British motor sports historian L.J.K. Setright, "for most of them to matter." So planners in Indianapolis decided to promote one big race on one special day when they got their new 2.5-mile banked track up and running. In 1909 they staged races at shorter distances, but as Setright wrote, "[e]ventually they decided on a distance of 500 miles (so that it could be concluded during daylight) and thus was born the richest, brightest, most ballyhooed, and occasionally most frightening, motor race in history."

A Brit who rarely said nice things about American racing is quoted here to give a sense of Indy's stature as it grew to be an iconic event in open-wheel racing. The American writer Robert F. Jones described the 500's domestic significance deliciously: "Years ago, on my first visit to Indy, the sky was blue and the sun shone down with that vibrant weight peculiar to the Middle West. This was an American homecoming—the greatest race in the world . . . the greatest spectacle in sport. Since its inauguration in 1911, Indy has become a happening, a transcendent event that dwells in the very bloodstream of America—a virus of velocity." In recent years, it's true, the Speedway and the 500 have changed. Stock cars have run at Indy in NASCAR's Brickyard 400 since 1994, an invasion that prompted Mario Andretti to say, "This would be like us running at Daytona. It's hallowed ground." And after the nasty split between CART (Championship Auto Racing Teams) and IRL (Indy Racing League) in 1996, the 500 had some down years, though most of the best open-wheel racers are now returning. They're coming back because it is a special race at a very special place. It is still the 500, at the Speedway.

Prologue to a Classic
Before there was a 500, there was a 100—in 1909, when these gents revved up for the first time in a dirt yard soon to be renovated as the Brickyard. The track was dangerous for all concerned, and before the first three-day race meeting ended, one driver, two spectators and two mechanics were killed. Organizers promised an improved track—pronto.

Indy's Genesis, Part I

Carl Fisher of Indianapolis, wanting to build a racetrack, wrote to a car magazine with his opinion that a longer, three- to five-mile track might make for more exciting racing than the one-mile standard then in use. He assembled backers and they bought 328 acres of land for $72,000. Their eventual plan was for a 2.5-mile track with banked turns. Lewis Strang, a winner in 1909, inspects a model of the oval, and Fisher himself drives members of the media round the big curves. In 1911 the race distance was set at 500 miles . . .

Culver Pictures

Indianapolis Motor Speedway (2)

Indy's Genesis, Part II

. . . Forty drivers, all of them Americans, entered that first contest at the classic distance. The winner seemed to be Ralph Mulford, who was given the checkered flag. But with so much at stake—$27,550—Mulford wanted to make sure he had counted right, and he proceeded upon three more laps. Meantime, Ray Harroun in No. 32 finishes his 500 miles and is declared the winner. Mulford's protests come to naught, as Harroun gets the money and a ceremonial quaff.

Culver Pictures

AP (2)

The Lay of the Land

The surface was initially crushed stone and tar, but that soon proved unstable, and late in 1909 the track was covered with 3.2 million bricks. Opposite: The bricks are still in evidence in 1947 as Walt Brown's Alfa gets emergency attention. Soon, though, all but the main straight was paved over with asphalt. Above, Bill Vukovich, in 130° heat, rides to victory in 1953. The Silent Serb took the laurels again in 1954 but was killed instantly in a crash in '55. At left, workers in '61 vacuum a literal ton of dust from the straightaway, which would finally be paved after that year's race. The 36-inch "Yard of Bricks" at the finish line is the only reminder.

Leonard McCombe

When Things Go Wrong

It was long a custom at Indy for spectators in the infield to erect scaffoldings to get a better view. In 1960 the homemade structure at left suddenly collapses during the parade lap, killing two and injuring more than 70. In 1964 reigning champ Parnelli Jones (above) was dueling for the lead when he pitted for fuel. As he pulls out, the car bursts into flames and he leaps for safety, clearing the rear tire. Jones said later that "even though I was burned and I was hurting, it broke my heart not to be running." It is chaos from the get-go in '66 (below) when half the cars were wrecked at the start.

Neil Leifer

Heinz Kluetmeier

A National Extravaganza

Memorial Day heralds the beginning of the American summer, and Indy is the event that gets the party off to a torrid start. Above, in 1963, some of the 250,000 spectators watch the drama unfold on a day when Parnelli Jones will snare his only title. At left, Johnny Rutherford in a Pennzoil Chaparral streaks to his third Indy win, in 1980. This was in the midst of a golden era, one that flourished for decades before CART threw down the gauntlet. It was an age studded with names like Foyt and the Unsers, Rodger Ward and Rick Mears. Rutherford summed up the desire that inflamed all those great drivers when he said, "I just wanted to go racing." A new, charismatic champion emerges in 2001 at the 85th Indy as Helio Castroneves (right) provides Penske Racing with its 11th Indy trophy, and to celebrate, the Brazilian-born driver takes a page out of Roberto Benigni's book when he triumphantly leaps on high to the delight of some 400,000 fans.

Robert Laberge/Allsport

DYNASTY The Chevrolets

cies, with fathers handing the wheel to sons.

An early racing family of renown sported one of automotive history's most famous names, Chevrolet, and therein lies a tale. Of three racing brothers—Louis, Arthur and Gaston—it was the eldest, Louis, who leant a mellifluous moniker to many millions of cars. He didn't intend to.

Born on Christmas day in 1878 in Switzerland, Louis emigrated to Montreal in 1900. Within six months, he was in New York City, working as a mechanic and racing cars. In 1905 the hard-charging European proved himself a force when he beat Barney Oldfield and all others on a cinder track in the Bronx, averaging nearly 70 miles per hour in a Fiat.

Two years later, Louis, now a racer of some reputation, met W.C. Durant, the founder of General Motors. This encounter was as fateful and perhaps as unfortunate as any in his life.

I f San Francisco Giants slugger Barry Bonds owes a debt to his major league dad, Bobby, and if golfer Davis Love III owes the same to Davis II, it is still safe to say that no sport in America is such a family affair as car racing. Its history is filled with brother acts and extended lega-

Louis relocated to Michigan and brought his kid brothers with him. All were racers; by 1910, Louis was a star. When Durant left GM he hired Louis to design a car under his own name. The result was a luxury auto priced high at $2,150. When Durant

At Indianapolis in 1915 the three mustachioed Chevys posed: Louis at the wheel; Gaston, far right; Arthur, by his side. When GM's Durant needed a chauffeur, he staged a race in Flint, Mich., to review the brothers' talents. He hired Arthur, the prudent driver. Louis (top left), the speed demon, was put on Buick's race team (above, in 1909).

sought to develop a cheaper Chevy as a counter-offensive to Ford in 1914, the proud Louis quit. He sold his stock to Durant for a pittance.

While Chevrolet the car went on to become an icon, Chevrolet the man went on to become a legendary but stupendously ill-starred racer and designer. At one point he set a track record at 111 miles per hour, but, routinely driving with unwise ferocity, he crashed so often that he spent some three years in the hospital during his 15-year career and saw four mechanics killed at his side. He won 27 major events including 10 in Indy cars, although never the 500. His youngest brother, Gaston, did win the Memorial Day classic in 1920 in a car designed by Louis, but the great family triumph was fleeting. Gaston died in a crash at the Beverly

Hills Speedway less than six months later.

Next, Louis and Arthur formed the Chevrolet Brothers Aircraft Company, but bad management sank the firm and led to enmity between the siblings. Louis tried aircraft again in partnership with Glenn Martin, but Martin got control of the firm when the stock market crashed in '29. While Martin enjoyed success with the Martin bomber engine, a machine largely of Louis's design, Louis met with yet more sadness. His eldest son died in 1934. That year, Chevrolet—the car company—which had rejoined with GM, had a pang of conscience and hired Louis as a consultant. Four years later a cerebral hemorrhage forced his retirement. He died in 1941 and was buried beside Gaston at Holy Cross Cemetery, not a stone's throw from the Brickyard.

OFF THE BEATEN TRACK

Wild times at the dunes, the drag strip and the demolition derby

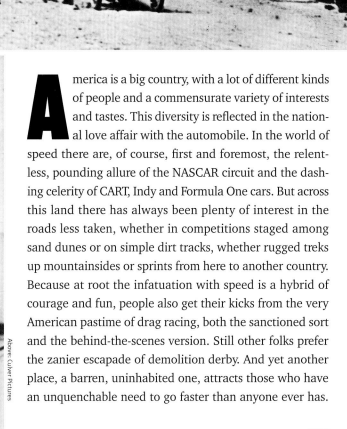

Anytime, Anyplace, Anyhow

The beautiful sand dunes at left are in the Imperial Valley near Yuma, Ariz., and in 1954 they attracted these desert hot-rodders to their graceful swirls. The dune buggies themselves look awkward but actually are quite spry, and if there is a tumble, the soft sand minimizes the boo-boos. Below: The storied Louis Chevrolet was always ready for all comers, as he proved when he took on aviatrix Ruth Law.

A merica is a big country, with a lot of different kinds of people and a commensurate variety of interests and tastes. This diversity is reflected in the national love affair with the automobile. In the world of speed there are, of course, first and foremost, the relentless, pounding allure of the NASCAR circuit and the dashing celerity of CART, Indy and Formula One cars. But across this land there has always been plenty of interest in the roads less taken, whether in competitions staged among sand dunes or on simple dirt tracks, whether rugged treks up mountainsides or sprints from here to another country. Because at root the infatuation with speed is a hybrid of courage and fun, people also get their kicks from the very American pastime of drag racing, both the sanctioned sort and the behind-the-scenes version. Still other folks prefer the zanier escapade of demolition derby. And yet another place, a barren, uninhabited one, attracts those who have an unquenchable need to go faster than anyone ever has.

Above: Culver Pictures

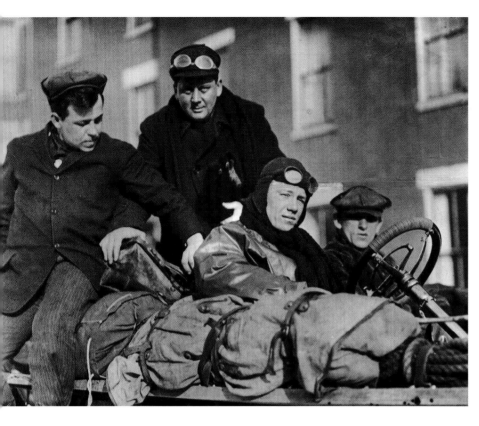

The Great Race

It had never been tried before and it has never been tried since. On February 12, 1908, six cars from four countries lined up in New York City's Times Square. As 250,000 looked on, a gold-plated pistol signaled the start of an around-the-world trip that would span 22,000 miles, 13,341 on land. The trek brought them across the U.S. and up to Alaska, then on to Japan, Siberia and finally to Paris. Little went as planned. The American entry, the Thomas Flyer (far right), was declared the winner, but only George Schuster (above, right) went the entire distance.

Four days in, the Americans enter Buffalo (above). First stop? The Thomas factory for alterations. The 60-hp Flyer had been taken right from the showroom floor and given minor modifications. In March they drive over the frozen Medicine Bow (right) in Wyoming. They often crossed rivers by fording or on trestles. Below, they zip through Nevada.

The Harrah Collection, National Automobile Museum (9)

The Flyer disembarks in Valdez, Alaska, but the snow proves impassable, so Vladivostok becomes the next staging area. Right: in Japan, en route to Russia.

A sampan starts the Flyer on its voyage to Vladivostok, where the race will resume. Right: At "Camp Hard Luck" in Manchuria, the team pits for repairs.

Before leaving Koenigsberg, Germany, the crew chats with some kids. At right, on May 22, after 88 days of driving, the winning Flyer is greeted by a crowd of Parisians.

Pikes Peak International Hill Climb (2)

Because It's There

The Pikes Peak International Hill Climb is America's second-oldest ongoing motor sport race, predated by only the Indy 500. Every summer, drivers of all sorts of vehicles flock to the fabled Colorado peak to test the 12.5-mile route, which features 156 turns as it rises 4,708 feet to its finish line at the 14,110-foot summit. And it's easy to see why they call it Unser Mountain: In the 50 years since Louis first won in 1934, seven members of the clan have taken 30 class titles, led by Bobby's 13. Counterclockwise from above: "Wild Bill" Bentrup in 1921; Al Rogers guides his Offy into a hairpin in '50; Nobuhiro Tajima nears the edge in 1992 but will end up a winner.

Is There a Doctor in the House?

Havoc is a staple ingredient in auto racing's winning recipe, a surefire spice that keeps the crowd alert.
Here are some exotic samples: The demolition derby (left, in 1964) is an event with very simple rules.
Everybody smashes into everybody else till only one car is running. That car wins. Derbies are de rigueur
at county fairs and often provide the coda to a night of competition in, say, midget racing (below, in 1938).
Because "doodlebug" tracks aren't banked, each turn holds the promise of sublime chaos. From the
sublime to the ridiculous, the gents above are hooded and thus driving blind in this 1932 outing. They
know the turn is coming because they "feel" the banked track. Joe Brusso in the DeSoto won.

Orlando Suero

Hank Walker (2)

Pedal to the Metal

Without doubt, one of the very first times that two Model A's pulled up next to each other, covert glances were exchanged, and the engines revved a little more, and then a little more, and then the brakes were let go . . . well, that was the first drag race, and that scene has been reenacted countless times at every red light in the country. It's a basic challenge: Who can go from here to there faster? No turns, no hills, just speed, like in the photos above and at right, in 1957. Some drags (the word means to stay in low gears as long as possible) are crackling, illegal events. Others are minutely regulated races like the one at far right in Cordova, Ill., in '63.

Bonneville Salt Flats: Built for Speed

In racing's earliest days, France, Belgium and the U.S. ruled the world of land-speed records. Then, from 1924 till 1963, drivers from Great Britain made speed their own little empire as they tore off a streak wherein they notched 20 out of 21 new marks. The two most legendary names are represented here. Malcolm Campbell set nine world records, the last (and Bonneville's first) in 1935 when he smashed the 300-mph mark in his famed Bluebird (left). Above, AAA officials inspect a 13-mile-long oil streak that Campbell used as a guideline. John Cobb set three records, including one in his Railton (opposite) that stood from 1947 to 1963.

The Right Stuff

On August 5, 1963, Craig Breedlove (above) decided it was time to bring the title back to America. Before then the fastest cars housed an internal combustion engine, but Breedlove's Spirit of America was a different breed of steed, in essence a land-bound jet that made the Californian an international celebrity when he snatched the record from John Cobb and surpassed 400 mph. But Breedlove wasn't done. In 1964 he topped the 500-mph mark, and then the following year he went 600.6 miles an hour in the Spirit of America Sonic I (opposite, top). Five years later, American Gary Gabelich, in his Blue Flame rocket car (center), took over the reign for 13 years. In 1997, in another jet, Britain's Andy Green shattered the record by an incredible 133 mph—breaking the sound barrier, too—when he drove 766.609 mph.

DYNASTY The Andrettis

A family affair: John, Michael, Mario and Jeff pose in 1991. Back in 1967 at Indianapolis, cousins Mark (Aldo's boy), Michael (Mario's), John (Aldo's) and Jeff (Mario's) don their racing suits and look to the future. Michael is still driving Champ cars, and John still pilots a stock car in NASCAR events. Mark is retired from racing; Jeff still dreams of a comeback. Opposite: Mario, in 1967.

Gigi Andretti, an Italian immigrant raising a family in Nazareth, Pa., in the late 1950s, didn't understand the fascination that cars held for his teenage sons, Mario and Aldo. Had he known they were sneaking to the outskirts of town to race on the Nazareth Speedway's half-mile dirt track, he would have put an end to it—or tried to. The boys realized this and kept their driving a clandestine affair. But in 1959, they could hide no longer. Aldo was in a bad crash over in Hatfield and was taken unconscious to the hospital. It was left to Mario to tell Gigi, who, Mario later recalled, "bounced me around the room like a football." Gigi was sure that the incident would knock some sense into his boys, and that if Aldo ever did come out of his coma, both he and Mario would find a safer hobby. But Mario, having been told by the doctors to stay by Aldo's bedside and whisper things that might motivate his comatose brother, was reciting a mantra about building a new race car. After 10 days, Aldo finally opened his eyes.

It took Aldo six months to recover, and he never again was the racer he had been before the wreck. Mario, on the other hand, went on to fast success, and when Gigi's pals at work started patting him on the back, congratulating him on his son's racing, even the patriarch came around.

Mario and Aldo were surely in no position to bounce their boys around the room when the kids came home and said, "Hey, Dad, gimme the keys." While Mario was building one of racing's greatest

Mario sits at the starting line of the Andretti dynasty, a man who started in stock cars and won the Daytona 500 but is an open-wheeler at heart.

careers—the only man to win the open-wheel Indy 500, the Daytona 500 in a stock car and the yearlong Formula One title in Europe; 52 Champ cars wins, second only to A.J. Foyt's 67; most Champ car poles (67) and laps in the lead (7,587) in history—while all this was happening, the next generation was revving up in midgets.

In the Indy 500 in 1992, both Mario and his younger son, Jeff, crashed. Mario broke some toes; both of Jeff's legs were shattered. As with Aldo, Jeff

George Tiedemann/Sports Illustrated

Jeff listens as Mario advises during Indy 500 qualifying in 1991. The stock Andretti, John (No. 43), has three NASCAR wins in nine years on the loop. He used to drive Champs as well.

raced again but never was quite the same.

Michael, by contrast, has won 42 times in Champ cars, though when he tried to replicate his dad's success in Formula One in 1993, he had a rough ride. Aldo's second son, Mark, raced karts as a kid, but the older boy, John, has found a home in NASCAR and—fittingly, considering the family heritage—became in 1994 the first man to race the Indy 500 and the stock World 600 in the same day, a stunt now attempted by at least a couple of superheroes each Memorial Day.

Michael's oldest son, Marco, is now racing karts. Eyes on the prize, he says his heroes include his grandfather, his father and, oh, yes, Juan Pablo Montoya. Marco's a throwback and right up-to-date, ready to take the legacy into the future.

David Taylor/Allsport

solating the birthplace of American stock-car racing is about as easy as passing an Earnhardt at Talladega. The sands of Daytona Beach? Well, that's a good place to start. But while Daytona reverberated with the roar of souped-up cars as long ago as the early 1900s, organization was lacking or laughable. By the 1930s, on dirt tracks throughout the South, on open roads through the hills of Pennsylvania or in California's wide open spaces, stock-car racing meant little more than kids and grown-up kids speeding wherever they could. The hottest stock races in the Carolinas during Prohibition were between bootleggers making deliveries in jury-rigged junks and feds sucking their dust. It wasn't until one Bill France started the National Championship circuit in 1946—which incorporated as the National Association of Stock Car Auto Racing in 1948—that jalopy races started looking like a league. Today, the league is legend.

NASCAR's Prehistory

To southeast Florida, where the street car's greatest shrine would one day rise in the form of a fast and famous racetrack, speed freaks made pilgrimages as early as 1903, questing after world records on the sands of Ormond Beach (above, in 1905) and going head-to-head at nearby Daytona (right and below).

Brown Brothers (3)

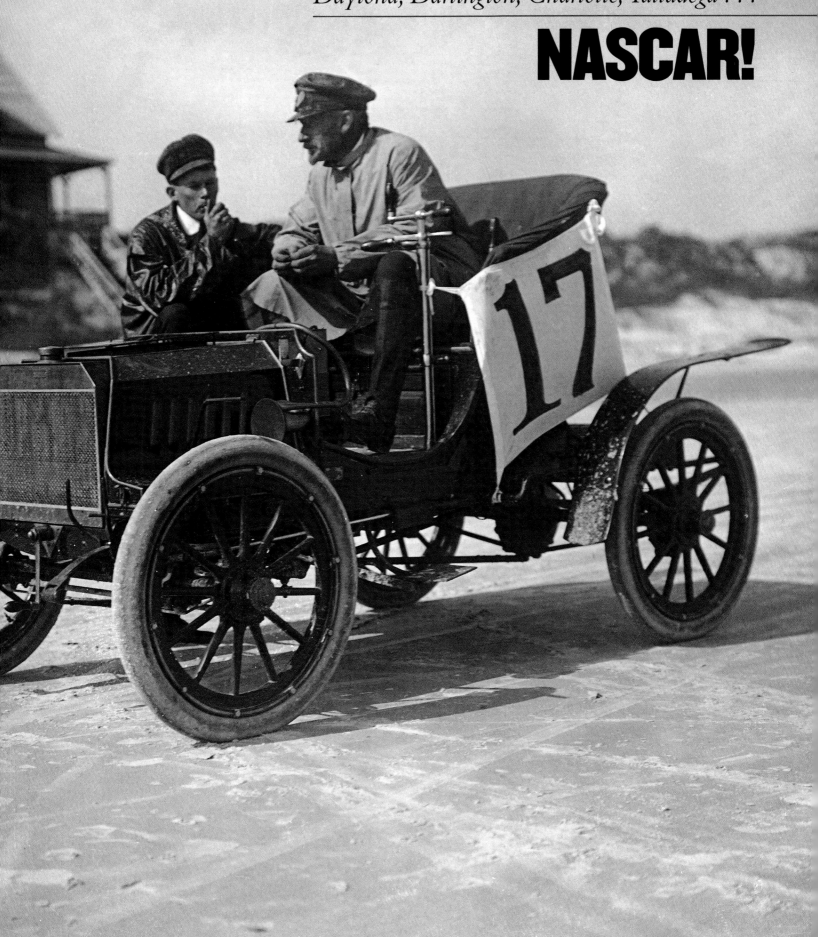

Daytona, Darlington, Charlotte, Talladega . . .

NASCAR!

Sea Change at Daytona

Sir Malcolm Campbell sped over the Florida hardpack at 330 mph in 1935, then said he would take his world-record attempts to Utah, a place more conducive to superfast times. Daytona's locals, addicted to speed, organized a 250-mile beach-road race for the next year. The $5,000 purse lured even Indy 500 champ Wild Bill Cummings. On race day, 20,000 fans show up to watch flag-waving beauties and sand-spewing lead-foots. But with a myriad of mired cars, the race itself is a bust. Milt Marion (bottom right) is said to have won, but no one is sure. Footnote: Bill France (center), a resident of Daytona for two years, finished fifth that day. A good driver, he was a better promoter, and by 1941 was organizing four annuals at the beach. World War II interrupted the racing but not France's train of thought.

Daytona Racing Archives

On the Beach

After the unfortunate experience of 1936, during which some turns became impassable due to soft sand, Bill France and others sought to improve their beach-road track. But in 1937 they had little money to offer, and only 21 drivers (19 of them Floridians) competed in the race. Things were starting to pick up a bit—those four races in 1941—when World War II intervened. It was after the war that Daytona became a happening scene (left, in 1950). Racers from Georgia, the Carolinas, Kentucky and Alabama came down, and fans showed up by the tens of thousands. France, encouraged, continued to organize and groom his racing enterprise. Before the decade's end, his efforts were manifested as NASCAR.

The Spread of NASCAR

NASCAR, synonymous with Daytona (opposite), branched out. Bill France's circuit invaded the North, where in 1947, Bob Flock, of the storied Flock flock of racers, won a 100-mile race on the vicious one-mile loop—not an oval but a circle known as "the big left turn"—in Langhorne, Pa. NASCAR went to Charlotte, N.C., for its first true all-stock race in 1949. It ran for the first time on a speedway at Darlington, S.C., where in 1958 (above) France glimpsed the future of his soon-to-be-paved Daytona. It made drivers stars: Buck Baker, Red Byron, Herb Thomas, Edward Glenn "Fireball" Roberts (right). Fireball won at his native Daytona in 1962, but died after crashing at Charlotte in '64.

Irma Combs Collection

Daytona Racing Archives (2)

AP

The Daytona 500

Even as Red Farmer was hitting a bump in the beach and taking flight during Daytona's annual marquee NASCAR race in 1953 (above), Bill France was beginning to plan and lobby for a slick asphalt superspeedway by the sea. His dream came true six years later, and in 1959 the inaugural Daytona 500 was staged. It was a "sweepstakes" race, the first and last time convertibles from that NASCAR racing division were allowed to join hardtops on the new, bumpless course. (Driving alfresco that day was 21-year-old Richard Petty, then a prince to his dad, Lee, the reigning NASCAR Grand National king.) The pristine race—not a yellow flag fluttered all day—featured the close-quarter racing that would become a NASCAR hallmark. The finish was a thriller, seemingly won by Johnny Beauchamp, who then received his spoils in victory lane. But Bill France and his aides spent several days with newsreels and photographs, including the one at right that shows (left to right) Joe Weatherly, who is two laps behind the leaders; Lee Petty; and Beauchamp. On Day Three the unofficial decision is reversed, and the trophy is handed to a happy Petty (right). NASCAR's modern era has begun.

Mike Staley Collection

Daytona Racing Archives (6)

He's a folktale made flesh, the bootlegger's boy from North Carolina who learned to drive like a demon by barreling over Brushy Mountain at two o'clock in the morning, trunk loaded with hooch and foot to the floor. A legend in Ingle Hollow and beyond, Robert Glenn Johnson Jr.—just call him Junior— was likely the best there ever was at the "bootleg turn," a maneuver wherein a runner, coming upon a tax agent's roadblock, spun his vehicle on a dime and vamoosed in the opposite direction. (Junior modified his technique very effectively when he developed a style of sliding into the curves of dirt tracks, then accelerating at midturn.) In Wilkes County, the admiring neighbors said he was as good with a wrench as he was at the wheel, building moonshine wagons that were faster than what was being

Junior loved to drive on dirt and sought it out even after he was a NASCAR star on asphalt. In 1956 on the rain-dampened sand of Daytona Beach, however, he can't hold the north turn in his No. 55 Pontiac, and goes through the spin cycle before fleeing the scene.

Junior Johnson Collection (2)

run at the speedway. "Moonshiners put more time, energy, thought, and love into their cars than any racers ever will," Junior said. "Lose on the track and you go home. Lose with a load of whiskey and you go to jail."

He did that once—went to jail, that is. "If a man needed to change, that was the place to change," he told the writer Tom Wolfe in 1964. "H'it's not a waste of time there, h'it's a good experience." Freed and reformed, Junior found that the precise talents that had built his fame on Brushy Mountain might do the same on the racing circuit. Wolfe described him in his classic essay "The Last American Hero Is Junior Johnson. Yes!" as "the hardest of all the hard chargers." He surely was that, a ferocious driver whose motto was "Win, wreck, or blow." As would Bobby Allison, Cale Yarborough and Dale Earnhardt in subsequent NASCAR generations, Junior built a devoted following throughout the South with his hell-bent-for-leather driving and a common-touch charisma. "Junior Johnson is one of the last of those sports stars who is not just an ace at the game itself," wrote Wolfe, "but a hero a whole people or class of people can identify with."

He won the second running of the Daytona 500 and 50 NASCAR races in all, including 13 of 36 starts in 1965. A year later he retired at age 35, turning back to his other love, tinkering. As a car owner, he saw his drivers win 119 races; Allison was his first racer, and Yarborough and Darrell Waltrip each won three Winston Cup titles for him.

Today, perhaps against the odds, Junior is a respected and respectable gentleman of North Carolina. He's still a hero, ever more a legend.

In 1935 agents seize 7,100 gallons of moonshine in a raid on Senior Johnson's operation (top left). Time passes, and the stills get back up and running. Junior gets nabbed in June 1956 (above), and spends 10 months in jail. (He'll subsequently be pardoned by President Ronald Reagan.) In 1960, Junior chills at Darlington (opposite). In '76 he declines Yarborough's offer.

Don Hunter

Southernmotoracing

DYNASTY The Unsers

Some of the clan gather in 1958 for one of Bobby's 13 wins at Pikes Peak. The victor stands at left, with the Unser Special beside him. Brother Al is on the right, next to parents Jerry Sr. and Mary Catherine. Below: The same year, brother Jerry flies over the wall at Indy. He would die in a crash there the next year. His son, Johnny, now an Indy driver, was seven months old.

Even if it were only for the Pikes Peak Hill Climb, those Unser boys would be one remarkable set of race-car drivers. Since the 1930s, this hardheaded breed has simply had their way on that prestigious but scary switchback dirt-and-gravel road. But, of course, that hill is only a part of the story for a family that has logged as many miles in the Indianapolis 500 as there are around the earth's equator.

The Unser family emigrated from Switzerland a little more than a century ago. The whole car thing kicked into gear when Jerry Sr. opened a garage in Colorado Springs. In 1936 he moved the business to Albuquerque, to take advantage of the growing traffic along Route 66. It wasn't an easy life. Jerry's son Bobby put it simply: "We were poor people." Once they found their proper calling, though, that would all change.

Louis Unser beat out eight other drivers in 1936 to win at Pikes Peak. Seven different Unsers have earned victories on the mount.

Al Sr. gets the first of his four Indy 500 wins, in 1970. Opposite, bottom: After the race, the champ gets a kiss from the matriarch.

Jerry Sr.'s brother Louis got the ball rolling with a win at Pikes Peak in 1934, and Jerry himself and another brother, Joe, who would be killed in 1929 testing an Indy roadster, also made their mark in racing. But the biggest contribution of this first generation was in creating the mold of determination,

toughness and hard work that would characterize Unsers yet to come. Among these were two of the greatest racers of all time, Bobby and Al Sr. Bobby was the older of the two, and before he was through, he won the Indy 500 three times. Bobby said it all one time: "Nobody remembers who fin-

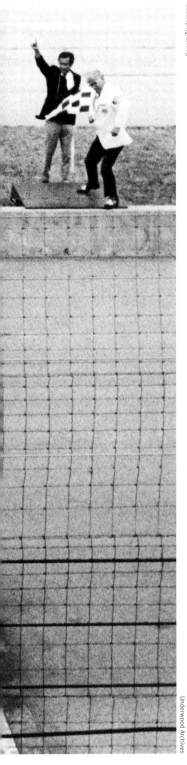

George Tiedemann

Underwood Archives

Big Al and Little Al compare notes at Indianapolis in April 1989. The son said of his father, "Dad taught me everything I know. Unfortunately, he didn't teach me everything he knows."

ished second but the guy who finished second." He and Al had another brother, Jerry, who was the 1956 national stock-car champ but crashed in a practice lap at Indy in 1959. Bobby was with him in the hospital the day before he died from his injuries. The talk wasn't about Jerry surviving, but that he might have a ride for Bobby. "That's the way the Unser family was in those days," said Bobby.

Only three drivers have won more Indys than Bobby— and one of them was his brother Al. "He's one of the top five racers who ever lived," Mario Andretti said of Al. "Nobody had race savvy like Al Unser in his prime." And "Little Al," his son, is a two-time Indy champ and a legend as well. To keep the fire going, Little Al's cousins, Johnny and Robby, have also driven at Indy. For this family, a hill wasn't enough. They had to own a brickyard, too.

Neil Leifer

WOMEN AT THE WHEEL

In a "man's world," the times they are a-changin'.

It's accepted wisdom that guys who drive race cars are pretty tough hombres. Out on the track, there is no quarter asked and no quarter given. So how tough must it have been—and still is, by most counts—for a woman to compete in this man's world? The answer is simple. Plenty tough. But they have been driving for a long time. In 1898, Genevra Delphine Mudge became the nation's first female driver, and the next year, she was racing. Other trailblazers included Camille du Gast and Canadian-born Kay Petre, who was dubbed Queen of Brooklands for her daring on that famed British oval. In the mid-'30s, she regularly competed in the 24 Hours of Le Mans. Yet it wasn't all that long ago when women weren't allowed in the pit or garage areas at the Indy 500. Now 22-year-old Sarah Fisher aims to win that event. She has the support. In 2001 fans voted her the IRL's most popular driver.

Brown Brothers

Pioneer Stock

Women have long had
a yen for racing and
competed against one
another and, when
permitted, with men.
In the early '20s, Grace
Leigh (above) became
the first woman to race
at Sheepshead Bay,
N.Y. Gwenda Hawkes
(right) drove two-,
three- and four-
wheelers in the '30s.

Born to Drive

In 1976, Janet Guthrie, (above, after qualifying for the Trenton 200) was the first woman to race in the Daytona and Indy 500s. Two years later, the former aerospace engineer finished ninth at Indy. Said Gordon Johncock, "She done a helluva job. The woman drove 500 miles with a broken wrist." Lyn St. James (left, in 1979) made her first of several Indy 500 appearances in 1992, placing 11th. Offtrack, she's a motivational speaker and does TV and charitable work.

Neil Leifer/Sports Illustrated

Everett Collection

Hear Me Roar

In 1965, Shirley Muldowney (above and top) became the first woman to race dragsters with the National Hot Rod Assn. In just a quarter of a mile those cars get up to 250 mph and then need a parachute to stop. Known early on as Cha Cha (she rejected the name in 1976 as trivializing), she was the first driver to win three world titles and was depicted in the 1983 flick *Heart Like a Wheel*. Craig Breedlove's wife, Lee (left), shared his passion for velocity. She set a women's land-speed mark of 308.6 mph in '65.

AN AMERICAN CLASSIC

Soap Box Derby is the Grand Prix of Gravity.

Jeff Iula Collection

F. Gordon Cook

The Graphite Kid
More than 65,000 turn out in 1946 to see Gilbert Klecan of San Diego take the crown. (The 14-year-old had rubbed his car—and his face—with graphite to "cut down wind resistance.") The drivers, who today range from age nine to 17, run three abreast.

The Depression was in full throttle in 1933, and folks were hungry for things to take their minds off the bleak reality. Then Dayton journalist Myron E. "Scottie" Scott saw three kids racing homemade engineless cars down a hill, and he arranged to photograph them and their pals the next week, with the winner getting a loving cup. The pictures were good, so a bigger race was held later that summer, and 40,000 came to watch. The following year, Chevrolet agreed to sponsor the first All-American Soap Box Derby, and champeens from 34 cities came to see who could coast the fastest. Tire companies quickly got the fever, and in 1935 the contest moved to Akron, a.k.a. Rubber City, where it has been held ever since. There are three different divisions, and rules govern the size, weight and cost of each car, which must be built by its driver. The quickest down the 954-foot course dons the traditional gold jacket.

Fire in the Tummy

Above: Clad in white uniforms and tin helmets, the 120 finalists climb the concrete runway in 1937 before a whopping 130,000 spectators. Robert Ballard of White Plains, N.Y., zoomed at 25 miles an hour to win not only the race but a four-year scholarship to any state university. Opposite: That certainly looks like a rocket coming down the track in 1959. Below, left: Bob Turner won the inaugural Derby, in 1934, and served as Parade Marshal at the Golden Anniversary in '87. Below, right: By 1997, some things have changed, the basics haven't.

EVERS LAUNDRY

DYNASTY The Pettys

Father to Son, Part I: Lee shares a smile with his son Richard. His other boy, Maurice, helped build engines for Richard throughout the King's career, which included a 1967 win at the Rebel 500 in Darlington (above). Opposite: Lee, Richard, Kyle and Adam in the spring of 2000, before tragedy struck.

Theirs is the first family in any sport to see four generations ascend to the major leagues. Theirs has been a journey marked by near-constant triumph, but also, recently, great sadness. After nearly a half century of checkered flags for the Pettys, the family's patriarch and its prodigy—the first and fourth generations of racers—died within weeks of each other in the spring of 2000. The old man was 86 and ailing, but the bright-eyed boy was only 19.

The legend starts with Lee, a mechanic in Level Cross, N.C., who used to abet his salary by winning wagers that he could outdrag the next guy on country roads. In June 1949 he drove the family car, a '46 Buick, to the first NASCAR race held at Charlotte, then drove it round the track until he rolled it. His fortune improved; he won the first Daytona 500, 54 other NASCAR races and three Grand National titles before retiring in 1964.

That year, one of his two boys, Richard, won at Daytona, and all sorts of mantles began to be passed. King Richard, as cordial as his dad was cantankerous but just as smooth and smart behind

the wheel, was, quite simply, the greatest stock-car driver
in history. In 1967, the year he broke
Lee's win record, he won 10 straight races and 20
in all. In 1971 he won 21 times, and in 1972 he
took his father's career Grand National title. By the
time he retired, he had won 200 races including
seven Daytona 500s, plus the yearlong Grand
National championship seven times. When asked
what he considered his greatest accomplishment
in racing, Richard said, "I guess in still bein' alive."

Father to Son, Part II: Richard and Kyle, 20, at Daytona in '81 (right). Above: Richard and Cale Yarborough duel at the 1984 Firecracker 400 at Daytona. Richard won.

Father to Son, Part III: Adam and Kyle in 1999. At Daytona in 2001, Kyle sheds a tear before climbing into his son's Chevy and piloting it in the 500. "I'm where he would have been," he said of driving No. 45. "I'm as close to him there as I am anywhere."

By the time Richard retired in '92, his son, Kyle, was already a NASCAR veteran. Lee drove No. 42 during his career and Richard's number was 43; Kyle would go on to win eight times and more than $11 million over 20 seasons in No. 44. Just as Kyle was ready to step back a bit, his son, Adam, was climbing into a No. 45 Chevrolet for Sprint. Successful in Busch series races, he then finished 40th in his first NASCAR event, a 500-miler in Texas, on April 2, 2000. Great-grandfather Lee heard the good news, then died three days later.

On May 12, Adam was in practice for a Busch event in New Hampshire when he hit the wall. Kyle, seeking ways to deal with his grief—the loss of his boy, his best friend—asked his sponsor, Hot Wheels, if he could forsake No. 44 and race No. 45 for Sprint. "Do what you think is best," they said. And so the Pettys drove on, their long and glorious campaign unhalted by death.

Jim Chini

Mark Kauffman/Sports Illustrated

Courtesy A.J. Foyt

f you were going to create a race-car driver, where would you start? Grit would be an essential ingredient. And he or she would have to be just plain tougher than everyone else, because if there is a fight, you might as well win. Ornery is good, when you're passing on the turn. Unshakable focus glued to lightning reflexes. You've got to drive mistake-free, which means driving smart. And you don't want to win, you have to win; there's no one who's going to take your rightful place. Add them all up, and you get A.J. Foyt, "the great-

Foyt started driving at the age of three. Two years later (left), with his name already on his race car, he was beating grown men. Above, c. 1961, on a dirt track; Foyt has been called the best midget-car racer ever. In 1964 (top left and bottom right) he drove to his second Indy 500 victory.

est driver that I ever knew," in the words of another legend, Junior Johnson. "The best all-around. He could drive anything, anywhere, anytime. Won in about everything he ever sat down in."

Anthony Joseph Foyt Jr. was born in Houston in 1935. His father was a Texas-tough mechanic. Said A.J.: "I never got that many whippings, but, whew, when I did, my daddy tore my ass up." The boy learned right from wrong, and that if you don't work harder than the other guy, he's going to beat you. So A.J. did the beating, at Indy (four times), at Daytona, at the 24 Hours of Le Mans. He is the only driver to win the three crown jewels of racing.

Bettmann/Corbis

STARS AND CARS

Hollywood has long loved the fast and furious.

Above: Pat O'Brien makes like Barney Oldfield (pages 20-21) as he ferries John Payne around in **Indianapolis Speedway,** a 1939 remake of an exciting 1932 Jimmy Cagney film (poster at right). **The Crowd Roars** was directed by Howard Hawks. Warner Bros. saved some dough by reusing a lot of its racing footage in the later offering.

Culver Pictures

Everett Collection (2)

James **CAGNEY**
Joan **BLONDELL**

THE **CROWD ROARS**

with ANN DVORAK
ERIC LINDEN
GUY KIBBEE
Story by HOWARD HAWKS
Adaptation and Dialogue by
SETON I. MILLER–KUBEC GLASMON
and JOHN BRIGHT
Directed by
HOWARD HAWKS
A WARNER BROS.
and VITAPHONE
Picture

James Garner takes to the reel wheel in **Grand Prix**, a 1966 flick that deftly laid in real sequences from European courses like Monza, Brands Hatch and Monte Carlo. The film made Garner a big racing fan, and he went on to have a team of his own. Garner's crew was chronicled in the 1969 film **The Racing Scene.**

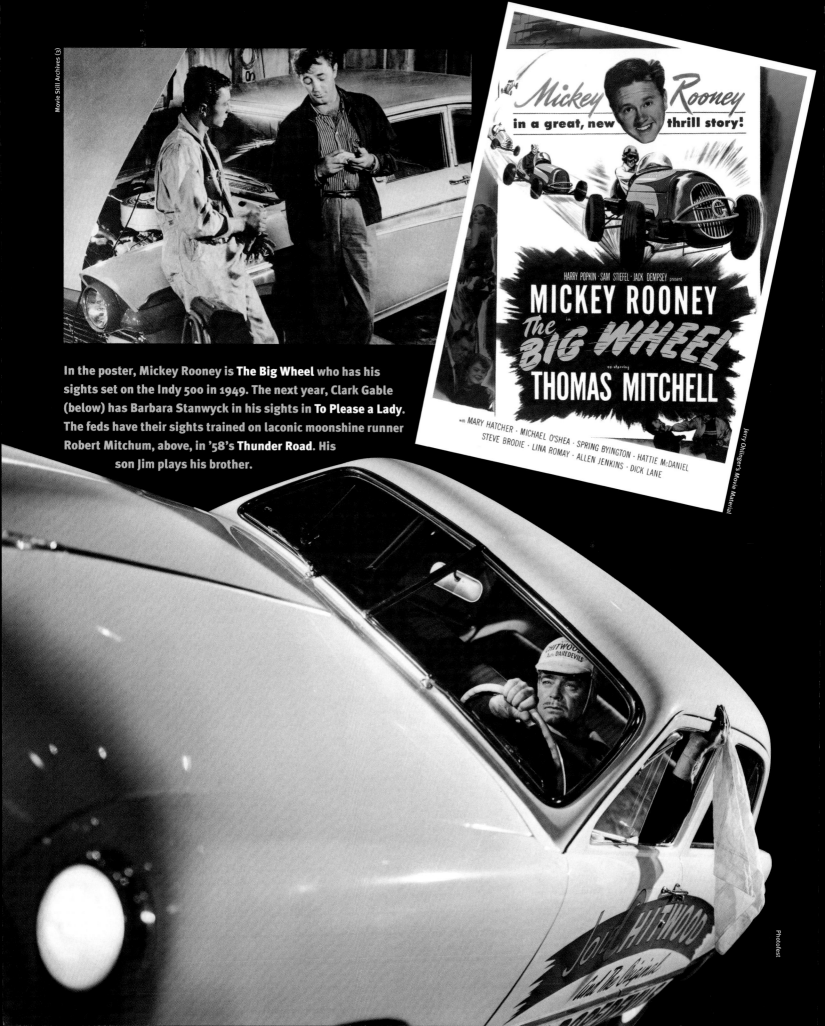

In the poster, Mickey Rooney is **The Big Wheel** who has his sights set on the Indy 500 in 1949. The next year, Clark Gable (below) has Barbara Stanwyck in his sights in **To Please a Lady**. The feds have their sights trained on laconic moonshine runner Robert Mitchum, above, in '58's **Thunder Road**. His son Jim plays his brother.

MICKEY ROONEY in a great, new thrill story!

HARRY POPKIN · SAM STIEFEL · JACK DEMPSEY present

MICKEY ROONEY
in
The BIG WHEEL
co-starring
THOMAS MITCHELL

with MARY HATCHER · MICHAEL O'SHEA · SPRING BYINGTON · HATTIE McDANIEL
STEVE BRODIE · LINA ROMAY · ALLEN JENKINS · DICK LANE

Wanna drag? A sensitive James Dean explains to a sensitive Natalie Wood why a guy needs speed in Nicholas Ray's 1955 classic, **Rebel Without a Cause.** Fay Spain in **Dragstrip Girl** might have pushed Dean aside to get behind the wheel herself in 1957. In George Lucas's 1973 film, **American Graffiti,** the California car culture is brilliantly captured. Below, on a lonely road, Harrison Ford and Paul Le Mat are waiting for a signal to pop the clutch.

Hollywood's Newest
TEENAGE STARS:

FAY SPAIN
STEVE TERRELL
JOHN ASHLEY
FRANK GORSHIN

DRAGSTRIP GIRL

An AMERICAN-INTERNATIONAL Picture

A GOLDEN STATE PRODUCTION · Produced by ALEX GORDON · Executive Producer: SAMUEL Z. ARKOFF · Screenplay by LOU RUSOFF · Directed by EDWARD L. CAHN

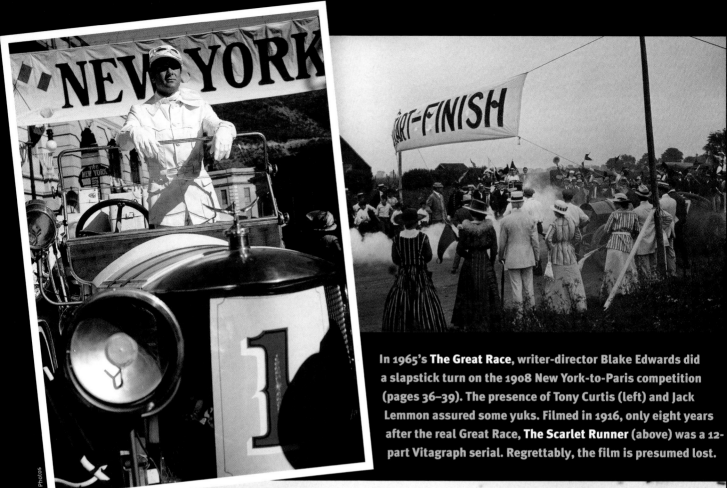

In 1965's **The Great Race**, writer-director Blake Edwards did a slapstick turn on the 1908 New York-to-Paris competition (pages 36–39). The presence of Tony Curtis (left) and Jack Lemmon assured some yuks. Filmed in 1916, only eight years after the real Great Race, **The Scarlet Runner** (above) was a 12-part Vitagraph serial. Regrettably, the film is presumed lost.

Elvis Presley *is* Lucky Jackson and Ann-Margret *is* Rusty Martin in **Viva Las Vegas** (1964). He wants to drive in the Las Vegas Grand Prix; she wants to be sure his motor's running, his mojo's working and his gears are well lubricated. They both succeed.

"Racing is the best way I know to get away from all the 'rubbish' of Hollywood," said Paul Newman, who first got the bug in 1972 when he made **Winning**. Above, he suits up at the Bonneville Salt Flats in '74. Mario Andretti drove for Newman and became his friend (below, in '94). Steve McQueen, who also used cars to escape the limelight, said that acting and racing "need the same absolute concentration."

NASCAR at 50
By the time Jeff Gordon (No. 24) outdueled Terry Labonte (No. 5) to win the Food City 500 in Bristol, Tenn., during NASCAR's 50th anniversary year in 1998, the circuit had long ago evolved from a gritty Southern carnival featuring a bunch of good-old-boy drivers to a coast-to-coast phenomenon with nearly six million fans flocking to Winston Cup races annually. A six-year network TV contract was in the offing as NASCAR sped toward the new millennium.

George Tiedemann

THE RISE OF NASCAR NATION

From humble stock comes an American passion.

Yes, early NASCAR was roughshod and regional, but founder Bill France negotiated the bumpy road efficiently. Then, in the late 1950s, Detroit, noticing that fans were buying car models raced by their heroes, moved south—and brought its checkbook. Much of America still thinks stock-car racing broke through about five years ago when the Kid—Jeff Gordon, he of the Tom Cruise looks—started turning up on the *Today* show to hobnob with Katie. But consider: By 1965, NASCAR was already the second most popular sport, by attendance, in the United States. And it hadn't yet waged its Northern offensive.

This assault would be gradual. To an itinerary of Spartanburg, S.C.; Birmingham, Ala.; and Hickory, N.C., NASCAR added, over time, Joliet, Ill.; Brooklyn, Mich.; Dover, Del.; and Loudon, N.H. The fans were attracted everywhere by the thunder of the cars, which have been able to reach 190 mph for 40 years now, and also by a host of stars every bit as human and accessible as the early characters, if better scrubbed. Richard Petty, David Pearson, Bobby Allison, Cale Yarborough and Dale Earnhardt developed fan bases within NASCAR Nation that were just as dedicated as Mickey Mantle's, Arnold Palmer's, Wilt Chamberlain's or Jim Brown's in the country at large. And once NASCAR was fully revved and rolling, there was no stopping it.

Challenging King Richard

Five years after Lee Petty won the Daytona 500, his son Richard (at far left) did too. At Daytona in '67, Mario Andretti (above, center; Bobby Allison is at front left) took the 500. Allison won 84 NASCAR events, often over Petty. Petty and David Pearson (below) ran one-two 63 times, Pearson winning 33.

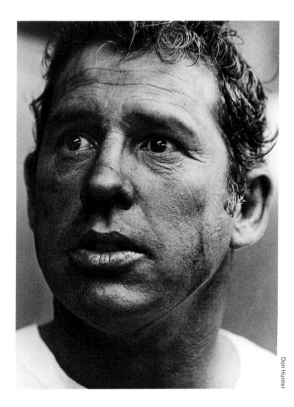

Hell on Wheels, Part I

Glory at the track is always hard-won. There was little available to Richard Petty in 1968 at the Daytona 500 when a brainstorm went bust. Petty hoped a vinyl top would prove an advantage, but when the roof came loose, his drag coefficient soared. During a pit stop the King himself takes hammer in hand, yet still finishes eighth. Eight years later—same place, same race—Petty and David Pearson dueled in the greatest NASCAR contest ever. After three lead changes on the final lap, they crashed exiting Turn 4. Both hit the wall; Pearson kept his engine running in No. 21, but Petty couldn't as he slid sadly onto the infield. Pearson coaxes his Mercury across the line (left), winning his first Daytona 500.

Hell on Wheels, Part II

In 1969 the tormented Lee Roy Yarbrough and his battered Ford came in first in Darlington's Rebel 400. Yarbrough crashed often and hard, developed a brain injury and a drinking problem, then, in 1984, died at age 46 after falling in a Florida mental hospital. In 1979, Dave Marcis's hand shows the effects of 500 miles' steering round Darlington. In '77, Frank Warren gets a little tenderness from his daughter after finishing 10th on a brutally hot day at Talladega.

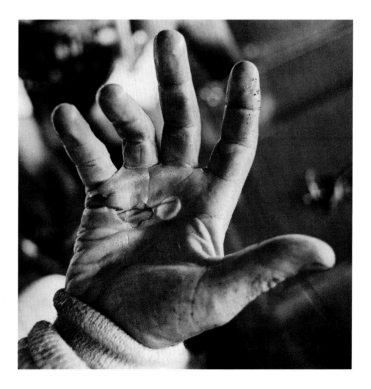

Hell on Wheels, Part III

Two of the best, most bullish drivers ever were Bobby Allison (left) and Cale Yarborough (right). They locked horns at the Daytona 500 in 1979. Bobby's brother Donnie (opposite, with mustache) had been leading when he and Yarborough crashed on the final lap, and Richard Petty went through to win. Bobby (in helmet) felt his brother had been wronged. Bobby later lost his two racing sons, Clifford and Davey, in car and helicopter crashes, respectively.

Rivals and Friends

Everyone liked Ned Jarrett, a gentlemanly racer who won two season series titles. In 1966 he triggered a fire extinguisher during his last race (below). Jarrett's son, Dale, competed in a NASCAR generation that included 84-time winner Darrell Waltrip (left, with his daughter, before a race in 1998) and Dale Earnhardt (right), seven-time Winston Cup Series champ. Lots of racers didn't like Ironhead's intimidating driving style but enjoyed his company off the track. Earnhardt and Waltrip parked their motor coaches side by side each weekend.

One Nation

The old circus was big, but the new one's huge, with attendance having doubled since 1990 (above, at Martinsville in 2001; left, at Atlanta in '99). A glimpse of NASCAR Nation: 40% of fans are women; 64% have attended college; 70% use the Net; 41% earn $50,000 or more; 38% live in the South, 17% in the Northeast, 45% elsewhere.

George Tiedemann

Many Allegiances

They fly the flags of the Union, the Confederacy and Anheuser-Busch (as here, at Daytona, in 1992). They wear the T-shirts of their idols, or mutilated T's of drivers they hate. (They spend $287 million a year on NASCAR merchandise.) They come (in 2000, 6.5 million of them to 36 Winston Cup races) to watch cars and to fight for their right to party.

Bill Frakes

The New Kids in the Grid

Jeff Gordon (above, in 1997, with Dale Earnhardt, and right, in 2001, winning at Watkins Glen, N.Y.) broke molds. He wasn't grizzled, he wasn't ornery—hell, he wasn't even Southern, having been raised in Indiana. Other New NASCAR successes included Dale's boy Dale Jr. and the Labontes, Terry and Bobby, below, with wife Donna after winning the Brickyard 400 in '00.

Brian Spurlock

George Tiedemann (2)

"He was my hero. Always has been, always will be," Dale (right, before his first Winston Cup race, in 1975) once said of Ralph (above). **"To this day I still use things he taught me."** Among the many traits Ralph handed down: toughness, spunk, aggressiveness and a particular penchant for perching on the bumper of the guy in front.

Before there was Ironhead, there was Ironheart. That was the original Earnhardt nickname and it belonged to Ralph, an expert mechanic and short-track racing god from Kannapolis, N.C. As tough and aggressive as his son would become, Ralph won more than 250 races in places like Monroe and Hickory, N.C., Columbia

and Greenville-Pickens, S.C. He won NASCAR's Sportsman Division championship in '56 and made a foray into Winston Cup, but didn't enjoy the big time, despite seven top-10 finishes in 1961.

Dale, born in 1951 in Kannapolis, was thoroughly his daddy's boy. He didn't take naturally to school—he would drop out in ninth grade—but loved being around cars. "I learned more in that garage than anywhere else," he said of his father's work space. Dale married at 17, and he and his wife had a son, Kerry. By the time he began his pro racing career at age 24 in 1975, Dale had a young family to support and, more than most drivers, was all business and no fooling. When strapped for cash, he would borrow from fellow racers, banking that he would win enough in Sunday's race for payback on Monday. That's pressure, and it made Earnhardt bear down, sometimes too hard. In one early-career

Gen-X Earnhardts include Dale Jr. (left) and Kerry, flanking their proud papa at the Michigan Speedway in August 2000. Kerry, currently in the Busch leagues, will race Winston Cup in 2002.

Ironhead, a senior citizen of the circuit, puts his feet up before finishing 16th in the California 500 in 1997. Less than four years later, he hits the wall at Daytona and NASCAR confronts the unthinkable. "No one ever expected Dale Earnhardt to die in a race car," says circuit chaplain Max Helton.

incident, he tapped and spun the car of dirt-track driver Stick Elliot. The word went out that Stick's mechanic had a gun and was looking for Ironhead. The pistol packer didn't find him, and the racer who would soon acquire a second sobriquet, the Intimidator, drove off to greater glory: 76 Winston Cup wins including, finally, the Daytona 500 in '98, plus a Petty-tying seven series championships.

In early 2001, Earnhardt's longtime PR manager, David Allen, said, "These past two years, having Junior on the track, we've all seen a marked change in Dale." Junior was Dale Jr., a son from Dale's second marriage and a rising NASCAR star. He had just finished second in the Daytona 500 on February 18, 2001, and his proud father was only seconds from the start-finish line when the first contact was made—with Sterling Marlin's car. The black No. 3 Monte Carlo veered right and plowed into the wall. "Dale, talk to us," the pit crew radioed. Silence. Earnhardt was dead at 49.

If anyone in America had been innocent of NASCAR Nation, they no longer could be in the wake of Earnhardt's death, as a massive outpouring of sympathy fell upon the family. Seven days later, Dale Jr. raced in Rockingham, N.C. Ironhead Earnhardt, Ironheart's boy, would have been proud.

The son rises: Dale Jr. was already a NASCAR winner before the events of February 2001, but in their aftermath he became a champion. Showing poise, confidence and determination, he wins dramatically when the Winston Cup Series returns to Daytona in July '01 (below). He also wins twice on the superspeedway at Talladega, a track Dad called his own.

THE FANS

Riveting Action, Start to Finish

Every year, tens of millions go to the track to watch, and be a part of, the spectacle of auto racing. The sights and sounds are unlike any other. Above: These fans along the starting line are among 130,000 at the '47 Indy 500. Mauri Rose took the honors in his Blue Crown Spark Plug Special; the famous old pagoda, which was taken down in 1956, provided a good view for officials and the press. Right: at the 1999 Brickyard 400, where Dale Jarrett has his No. 88 Ford on the road to victory.

No Fence-sitters Here

Racing has every manner of allure for its sundry fandom. The family and friends at left are picnicking at the fifth annual Pebble Beach, Calif., sports-car races in 1954. The route carries the racers along the enchanting 17-Mile Drive. The family above are ensuring that they will always remember their trip to the 1996 Southern 500 at Darlington. Used tires can be bought at $10 per after the race, and fans vie for those of their heroes. The winner there was Jeff Gordon, seen at right autographing a cap at the Pocono 500 in 2001.

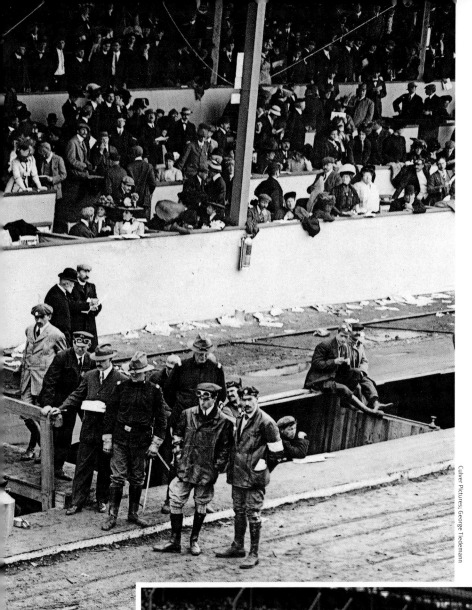

IN THE PITS

Fill 'er Up—and Fast

Once upon a time they were, well and truly, pits. During the 1908 Vanderbilt Cup competition, extremely idle supporters look on as driver and mechanic service their own car. Much has changed by the time Al Unser Jr. pits at Indy in 1991. In open-wheel racing the driver stops directly on marks painted on Pit Lane so his mechanics can swoop to their appointed positions. The car is jacked up, the fuel hose locked on, the old wheels taken off, the new ones put on, the car is lowered, the hose is disengaged and—*zoom!* Wheels can weigh 85 pounds and so, in recent years, pit crews have been put through daily practice sessions and enrolled in agility and weight-training programs. Since it is easier to gain track position with fast pit stops than by trying to pass cars in action, lowering times is vital. A quick look at a relatively young racing circuit, NASCAR, illustrates the premium now put on pit work. In the 1950s, a pit stop could take four minutes. Today, 25 seconds is slow.

Rush Hour on Skid Row

Richard Petty was an early NASCAR evangelist for faster pit stops, and Jeff Gordon's superfit "Rainbow Warriors" hastened all others to the gym in the '90s. It is best to pit under a yellow light, since the race isn't racing off without you. In 1999 during the Las Vegas 400, circumstances result in a traffic jam on Pit Lane.

George Tiedemann (2)

At the Track, Part III

CRASH!

A Part of the Game

Ever since only Frank Duryea and one other driver
were able to get their cars to the finish of the Chicago-
Evanston rally in '95—that's 1895—crashing and
conking out have been part of American auto racing.
Cynics say that's why many fans go to the track: to see
the crashes. That's probably not so, but crashes are
nevertheless a spectacular, if horrific, part of the
sport. Racing organizations have long been reluctant
to keep accurate statistics on accidents and,
particularly, fatalities—with one eye on the image of
the game and the other on insurance costs. But an
insider says it's a safe bet that there have been
approximately 50 deaths a year over a period of 70
years, which would mean 3,500 have died in that time.
Two who did not: Eddie Pullen in the 1914 Vanderbilt
Cup Race (right) and Robert Pressley, framed by
flames at a NASCAR race in Bristol, Tenn., in 2000.

Hulton-Deutsch/Corbis; Sam Sharpe (bottom)

Walter T. Chernokal/Chester Times

Jim Gingrich

Slipping, Sliding and Soaring

The area behind the south turn of Daytona's beach-road course becomes a sandy junkyard in 1955 during a 100-mile NASCAR Sportsman Class race as Pee Wee Hornsby's 53A joins a half dozen confreres. Right: At Langhorne Speedway outside Philly in 1957, Charles Musselman departs a 100-lap race on the 80th lap. He's lucky that his harness has broken since his airborne exit leaves him bruised but whole. Also fortunate is Salt Walther at the 1973 Indy 500 (below). His crash results in serious burns, but he'll race again the next year.

AP

IN VICTORY LANE

Bring On the Smiles

The thrill of victory . . . there's nothing quite like it, as is clear in these pages. That's one happy gaggle of Americans at left, the Rohrer family from Rochester, N.Y., which is gathered around the winner of the 1955 All-American Soap Box Derby, 14-year-old Richard. Above, Rodger Ward (right) finished in second place in the 1964 Indianapolis 500, but what the heck, he had already won twice there, in 1959 and '62, so he is reasonably content to play the gracious also-ran and congratulate the day's winner, A.J. Foyt, in the garage. For his part, Foyt, buoyant with the second of his four Indy crowns, is more than happy to doff the garland of roses and share it with the bemused runner-up.

To the Victors Go the Spoils

Clockwise from left: With the Indy 500 trophy behind him, Mario Andretti endures a buss from team owner Andy Granatelli in 1969; actress Carole Landis prepares for '47 winner Mauri Rose; another screen lovely, Virginia Mayo, works the crowd in '56 as Pat Flaherty makes do with milk; Miss Georgia gets Fireball Roberts gaga after the '60 Dixie 300; that same year, things were great for Jack Penwell till he saw the photographer and remembered his wife back in Tulsa.

Life Is Good

After a race, the rest of the field can go off by themselves and figure out what went wrong, but the winner is going to have a lot of company. Of course, Rick Mears (opposite) is used to that sort of thing by 1984, as he pulls in with his second of four Indy 500 titles. Mears and his Pennzoil Z-7 won by a two-lap margin. Both of the guys above are familiar with the taste of triumph. That's Al Unser Jr. getting a shower from Big Al after winning the Budweiser Cleveland Grand Prix in 1985. The old man didn't do too bad either, finishing third. At right, showgirls endow Sterling Marlin with the scarlet hallmarks of victory after the 2002 UAW DaimlerChrysler 400 in Las Vegas.